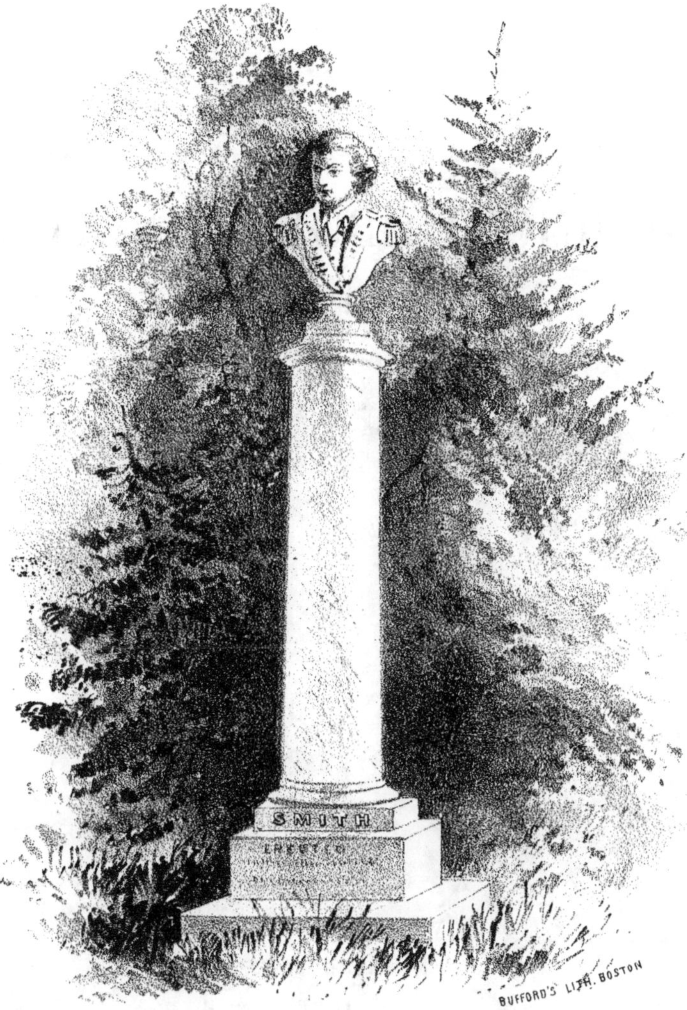
SMITH
ERECTED
BUFFORD'S LITH. BOSTON

I

HARMONY GROVE CEMETERY

SALEM, MASS.

PUBLISHED BY

G. M. WHIPPLE AND A. A. SMITH,

SALEM, MASS.

1866.

Salem Observer Press.

CONTENTS.

HARMONY GROVE CEMETERY.

TWENTY-FIVE years have elapsed since these grounds were consecrated to the sacred uses of a rural cemetery. Nearly an entire generation have passed away; many, who were present and who took a part in that interesting occasion are gone, their mortal remains lie buried within these hallowed precincts,—their memories will long live for their many virtues and for their zeal in works of public improvement; may their examples and precepts long continue to remind successive generations of their duty in the preservation of these memorials of the past.

This retreat had long been familiar to the lovers of nature, who were attracted thither not only by the beauty and diversity of the scenery, which presented in pleasing combination, the rocky cliff, the woody knolls, the sheltered valley with shady groves, sunny slopes and verdant plains, but by the great variety of flowering plants which there abound, and by the harmony of the feathered songsters which have always enlivened by their notes the beautiful grove which owes to them its name. Fortunate that the woodman's axe had spared these trees, and that the former proprietors of the soil had preserved so much of its pristine beauty and freshness that it should come to us with the features requisite, of all others, for this object.

The organization of Horticultural and kindred associations in New England, (the older ones date their origin some thirty or forty years or more since), awakened and have continued to exert a great influence in nurturing a taste for the pleasures of rural life, and in directing attention to a more refined culture and to the embellishment of our country residences with a happy combination of trees, shrubs, lawns and gardens; thus adding a new and very agreeable feature to our scenery and contributing much to the amenities of our New England home. The influence of these associations would naturally direct the minds of the people to bestow a corresponding care in the selection of places to deposit the remains of dear and beloved friends, and to cover the graves with verdure and to adorn them with flowers,—appropriate emblems of pure and holy feelings.

In accordance with the prevalence of these sentiments elsewhere, influenced in part by the limited extent and crowded state of the city burial grounds, the idea of establishing a rural cemetery was first suggested. It was deemed desirable to procure for this purpose, a situation, which, either by its natural beauties or by receiving the ornament and improvement that art could bestow, might afford that retirement which is pleasant to associate with places of this character; removed from the centre of population, yet sufficiently near to be always easy of access; of such extent to prevent its soon becoming

II.

crowded, and so arranged that the remains deposited, would never at any future period be disturbed; the whole to be secured by Legislative enactments from intrusion or violation and from being appropriated to any other object.

With this purpose in view, at the suggestion of Mr W. H. Foster, some gentlemen, interested in the project, assembled by the invitation of Mr Pickering Dodge, at the Lyceum Hall in this city, in February, 1837. About fifteen persons assembled, among whom were Messrs. Francis Peabody, Charles Lawrence, A. L. Peirson, Francis Putnam, William P. Richardson, Henry Wheatland, Pickering Dodge and William H. Foster. As several of the clergy, especially the Rev. Messrs. Brazer, Wayland, Upham and Thompson, took much interest in the project, it is probable that some, if not all, of these gentlemen were likewise present. But one opinion was expressed at this meeting as to the expediency of establishing a Rural Cemetery, and several situations were suggested as suitable for the purpose. It was, however, decided, before proceeding further, to call by advertisement in the newspapers a public meeting of all friendly to the undertaking.

Accordingly, in consequence of a notice published in the Salem Gazette of Feb. 24, 1837, a meeting was held at the Lyceum Hall, on that evening, which was organized by the choice of Francis Peabody as Moderator, and William H. Foster as Clerk. After discussing the plan of the proposed Cemetery, its probable cost, and the merits of the different localities suggested, in which discussion Messrs. Peabody, Peirson and others were engaged, the meeting selected a committee consisting of Messrs. P. Dodge, W. H. Foster, A. L. Peirson, H. Wheatland and F. Putnam, to ascertain on what terms the different sites alluded to could be procured, in what manner the funds necessary for the purchase could be raised, and to obtain the refusal of such situation as they should decide, after examination, to be best suited for the intended purpose. This Committee were to report, in relation to the various subjects committed to them, at an adjournment of the meeting.

After examining various sites, both in North and South Salem, the Committee came unanimously to the conclusion that Harmony Grove possessed all the requisites for the contemplated purpose; they ascertained the price for which it could be purchased, obtained a refusal of the land, took some steps to raise the funds necessary for the purchase, and then notified the meeting to be held on the evening of May 12, 1837, at the Lyceum Hall to hear their report.

The evening of May 12, 1837, is memorable in the annals of New England as the one on which the Banks of Boston and this vicinity were compelled to suspend specie payments. The gloom produced by that event and the pecuniary embarrassment of the country, together with the pressing and indispensable engagements on that evening of several of the gentlemen who had taken most interest in the undertaking, prevented the attendance of

BUFFORDS' LITH. 313 WASH. ST. BOSTON.

III.

PUTNAM
J. H. BUFFORD'S LITH. BOSTON.

any at the meeting, but the chairman and two or three others; the project was, as by common consent postponed to a more convenient season.

Though suspended, this project was not abandoned. The belief in its necessity still continued and led to new efforts for its attainment. In consequence of the crowded state of the Public Burial Grounds, the city authorities had for some time been considering the expediency of providing further accommodations for the interment of the dead. The Mayor, Hon. Stephen C. Phillips, early in the year 1839, called their attention to this subject and instituted some enquiries with the view of enlarging the present burial grounds by the purchase of additional land for the purpose. Before any action was taken, he was informed of the doings of the committee of Feb. 1837, and again called public attention to the subject of a Rural Cemetery, and was greatly instrumental in its establishment upon a permanent basis; he entered into the project and lent his aid with all that ardor and energy which characterized the discharge both of his public and private duties; he suggested to the city authorities in a communication to that body Sept. 9, 1839, the expediency of their uniting in the undertaking, and thus obviating the necessity of enlarging the present grounds or procuring a new place of sepulture. These suggestions were favorably received by the City Council and such assurances given as led to an arrangement which was subsequently authorized and carried into effect.

In consequence of a notice, published in the newspapers, a meeting of those friendly to the establishment of a Rural Cemetery, was held at the Lyceum Hall, on the evening of the 3d of September, 1839; Mr. S. C. Phillips was appointed chairman and Mr. W. H. Foster, secretary. At this time, the object of the meeting was fully stated by the chair, a verbal report of the doings of the committee formerly chosen on the 24th of Feb. 1837, was made by their chairman, Dr. A. L. Peirson, and the form of an agreement to obtain subscriptions for a loan of money to carry into effect the objects of the meeting, was submitted by William H. Foster, to whose early and continued zeal and interest in its accomplishment, to the present time, the cemetery is much indebted for its establishment and its present prosperous condition. It was then *voted*, That Messrs. Wm. H. Foster, George Wheatland and Edward H. Payson of Salem, and Fitch Poole of Danvers, be a committee to obtain such subscriptions, and that Messrs. Stephen C. Phillips, Joseph S. Cabot, Ephraim Emmerton, William Sutton, and William H. Foster be the Trustees of the funds thus raised.

Subscriptions to a sufficient amount having been obtained to authorize the undertaking, a meeting of the subscribers to the fund was held on the 6th of Sept., 1839, of which Mr. Phillips was chairman and Mr. W. H. Foster clerk. At this meeting Messrs. Francis Peabody, Joseph S. Cabot and George Wheatland were chosen a committee with discretionary power to purchase a portion of the ground, now owned by the corporation. The committee purchased eight acres of Mr. George W. Rugg for twelve

IV

hundred dollars, and fourteen acres of Mr. John G. Wilkins for sixteen hundred dollars; two acres and a half of Mr. Jacob Putnam for four hundred and fifty dollars; six acres of Mr Joshua Buxton for eleven hundred and seventy dollars; and about seven acres of Messrs. Joseph Buxton and Solomon Varney for nine hundred dollars. Afterward, an exchange of a small part of the land purchased of Joshua Buxton was made with Ichabod Nichols, for a piece of nearly similar extent in order to improve thereby the shape of the grounds; and with a view of straightening the northern line of the cemetery a portion of that purchased of Wilkins, Joseph Buxton and Varney, was sold to Stephen Nichols. The quantity of land purchased and retained for the cemetery at the time of its consecration, was about thirty-five acres, and cost five thousand three hundred and twenty dollars.

At a subsequent period there have been purchased of Ichabod Nichols one and one quarter acres for five hundred and fifty dollars, of Sam'l Crane eight and one quarter acres for thirty-two hundred dollars, of R. W. Merrill one and a half acres for eighteen hundred and seventy-six and a half dollars, of E. S. Upton one and a half acres for nineteen hundred dollars; also the city of Salem interest for two thousand. Total number of acres 47½; cost $14,849.50.

At a meeting September 20, 1839, Messrs. F. Peabody, J. S. Cabot, A. L. Peirson, S. C. Phillips, and J. C. Lee were appointed to collect the subscriptions to the fund for the cemetery, to determine upon the form, and to issue receipts to the subscribers for the amounts so furnished by each, and to see that proper conveyances of the lands purchased were made to the Trustees of the fund in a form to be determined by the committee. The lands were held by the Trustees until an act of incorporation was obtained.

At a meeting of the subscribers to the fund held Oct. 4, 1839, Messrs. F. Peabody, J. S. Cabot, S. C. Phillips, A. L. Peirson, J. C. Lee, G. Wheatland, W. H. Foster, P. Dodge, William Sutton and Fitch Poole were chosen a general committee of superintendence, with authority to take such measures to carry into effect the intentions of the subscribers, as they might think proper; of this committee, F. Peabody was chairman, and W. H. Foster, clerk and treasurer.

The committee secured the services of Alexander Wadsworth of Boston who made a topographical plan and laid out the grounds with walks and avenues. A rustic arch and gateway of stone was constructed at the eastern entrance, from designs by and under the directions of Francis Peabody, one of the principal originators of the cemetery, and whose services on the committee, for his taste and judgment have been of very great importance; other works were commenced and prosecuted, until winter put a stop to further operations.

An act was passed by the Legislature of 1840, creating certain persons named therein, and all those who should become purchasers of lots in the cemetery, a corporation, to be called the HARMONY GROVE CEMETERY with all the rights and privileges usually belonging thereto. This act secures to purchasers of lots the quiet and uninterrupted

V.

enjoyment of the same, and punishes with severe penalties any trespasses or violation of the grounds. It was accepted at a legally notified meeting held on the 29th of February, 1840, of which F. Peabody was moderator and W. H. Foster, clerk. A committee consisting of Messrs. Phillips and Wheatland, was appointed to draw up and report Rules and By-laws for the government of the corporation. At a subsequent meeting on the 16th of May, 1840, the By-laws reported by this committee were adopted, and the corporation duly organized by the choice of officers.

With the return of Spring, the work on the cemetery was renewed and by the first of May, was in such a state of forwardness as to render it certain that the lots would be ready for sale early in the ensuing month, and the grounds so far prepared for their intended object that the consecration might take place at that time. At a meeting of the committee on the 2d of May, it was voted that the consecration should take place on the first Wednesday in June, which time, however, was subsequently altered to Saturday, the 13th day of June, and that the Hon. Daniel A. White be requested to deliver an address, and the Rev. Dr. Brown Emerson of Salem, and Rev. C. C. Sewall of Danvers, be invited to perform the religious services suited to the occasion.

The corporation having been legally organized, the land purchased for the cemetery and which had been held by the Trustees of the subscribers of the fund for its purchase, was in accordance with the terms of the trust conveyed to the corporation. In accordance with the arrangements between the City Council and the Trustees, for two thousand dollars, the corporation conveyed to the city nearly three acres of land, included in five lots in different portions of the grounds, to be used by the city for the burial of the dead in graves only. In 1850, the corporation reimbursed to the city the two thousand dollars and the land was rëconveyed to them.

The consecration of the cemetery, took place on Sunday, June 14, at half past five o'clock, P. M.; it having been postponed from Saturday the 13th, in consequence of the unpleasantness of the weather. Seats to accommodate three thousand persons had been prepared on a gentle slope, gradually ascending from Dell avenue, the ground there forming a natural amphitheatre, particularly well adapted for this purpose; a rustic bower, for the accommodation of the gentlemen engaged in the consecration, was erected at the foot of the slope, where the address was delivered and the other services of the day performed.

The day was one of the finest days in June, clear, calm and bright; a gentle breeze, loaded with the perfume of the locust blossoms, tempered the heat of the sun, while the showers of the previous day had imparted to the grass and the foliage of the trees, tints of the deepest and richest green.

The services consisted of prayers by the Rev. Dr. Brown Emerson of Salem, and Rev. Charles C. Sewall of Danvers; an address by the Hon. Daniel A. White; an original hymn by Rev. Dr. James Flint, and an original ode by Mr. William Wallace Morland, of Salem, furnished by these gentlemen at the request of the Trustees, the hymn having been read by Rev. Dr. Flint, and the ode by Rev. Mr. Wayland. At the close of the services, Old Hundred was sung, with great effect, the whole audience joining in a hymn written for the occasion by Nathaniel Lord, Jr. Esq., of Ipswich. The music, which was entirely vocal, was under the direction of Mr. Jacob Hood. The services were of a very impressive character and listened to with silent interest, by the immense audience which filled every seat and thronged all the spaces within sound of the speaker's voice. From the most accurate calculation which could be made, it was supposed that at least from six to eight thousand persons were present on the ground; yet notwithstanding the greatness of the numbers and denseness of the crowd, perfect order was maintained.

On the Tuesday succeeding the consecration, 16th of June, the lots were offered for sale at public auction, by Mr. Gilbert G. Newhall the auctioneer, about three hundred having been surveyed and prepared for this purpose; this day, seventy-seven lots were disposed of, at premiums varying from one to twenty-five dollars. The whole amount of the bonus thus received, on the choice of lots was five hundred and forty-two dollars. During the next succeeding few days, thirty-six lots more were sold at the minimum price of ten cents per square foot, making one hundred and thirteen lots that were sold at the opening of the cemetery.

The cemetery was formerly situated within the limits of the town of Danvers, but the Legislature of 1840, passed an act so altering the boundaries of the city of Salem and the town of Danvers, that the whole of the cemetery and the three avenues which lead to it, were placed within the limits of the city of Salem. About the same time the town of Danvers constructed a way from the principal street in that town, at the foot of Poole's Hill, to enter the cemetery on its western boundary.

The grounds of the cemetery are peculiarly well adapted to their intended purposes, the varied soil and aspect are favorable to the culture and growth of the different kinds of trees and shrubs that will endure this climate,—the attainment of this object, more especially the collecting of those that are indigenous to New England, has always been one of the prominent designs of the Trustees.

Few places combine so great a variety within equally narrow limits. Here are extensive views, picturesque dells, and rough and craggy rocks protruding from the sides of steep declivities, covered with moss-grown trees; here are open plains, shady groves, and sunny glades, as if nature had framed this spot for the very purposes for which it was consecrated. Here in the early Spring, the feathery tribes will be heard heralding with their melodious songs the dawn of day, and warbling forth their latest vesper hymns. Here the squirrels will resume their gambols and chirping among the branches, now that the truant school boy is not permitted to molest or disturb them, the butterflies will be flitting in the Summer sunshine sipping nectar from every opening flower. In fine all nature, living in unison with the peace and solitude there predominant, will unite in one grand choral song of praise to Him, the maker and ruler of all.

VII .

NOTICES OF VIEWS.

I.

A marble column surmounted by a bust of Washington—situated at junction of Valley Avenue and Angelica Path—on the base are the following inscriptions:—

Front.
Erected by his fellow citizens.
In memory of
Jesse Smith
born April 13, 1756
died June 4, 1844

Right side.
The Last Survivor
of the Body Guard of
Washington,
and through life
in Peace as in war
his worthy follower.

Left side.
A Patriot of the Revolution:
Serving in the army
throughout the war:
Present at the battles of
Concord, Lexington, Bunker Hill,
Brandywine, Germantown, Monmouth.

Rear.

Buried by his side,
lie the remains of
Sallie Smith
Wife of Jesse Smith
born Jan'y 15, 1761, died August 21, 1840.

At the commencement of hostilities in 1775, Mr Smith resided in Lincoln, and belonged to a company of Minute Men. He was called out on the morning of the 19th of April, 1775, marched to Concord and followed the retreating British army to Charlestown. April 21, he enlisted for eight months and was in the battle of Bunker's Hill. He served out his enlistment and then again enlisted for one year, and was drafted into Gen. Washington's First Foot Guards. In Dec., 1776, he enlisted for three years in a company of Horse, as Washington's First Horse Guards. Leaving the army he came to Salem and entered on board of a privateer, was taken prisoner and confined in Mill Prison till the close of the war. He was afterwards a highly intelligent shipmaster.

II.

Matthew Adams Stickney. Marble Obelisk.
Lot 4. Grove Avenue.

Here are interred,

Mary Elizabeth Stickney, first wife of Matthew A. Stickney, born in Salem, Dec. 17, 1810, was the daughter of

VIII.

Caleb and Betsey (Winchester) Smith. She died May 9, 1834, and was buried in the old Danvers Burial Ground, and was rëinterred November 4, 1840, by Matthew A. Stickney, in this lot, where he had erected, September 1, 1840, the first marble monument in the Cemetery.

Lucy Waters Stickney, Second Wife of Matthew A. Stickney, born in Salem, November 10, 1816, was the daughter of John and Eleanor (Shales) Waters. She died February 13, 1847, and was buried February 15, 1847, in this lot.

III. & III.*

In this enclosure, on Highland Avenue, corner of Maple Avenue, are interred the remains of Jacob Putnam and several of his children.

Jacob Putnam was born in Danvers, on the 17th of November, 1780, son of Stephen and Susanna (Herrick) Putnam. He came to Salem in early life, and engaged in business, which he conducted through a long life with eminent success. He died on the 18th of January, 1866.

The plan numbered III* is the design for a monument now in process of completion to be erected to his memory. The Base and Dies are composed of finely finished Quincy granite, with panels of marble, and the shaft with richly executed vases is also of marble. The height of the whole is about twenty feet. It is being executed by Mr. Garrett Barry Jr., from designs by Mr. R. D. Wilkie.

IV.

In this enclosure, situated on Beech Path, are several monuments, one of which was erected to the memory of P. D. ALLEN, and the following inscriptions are inscribed thereon:

Front.

Pickering Dodge Allen,
Lieutenant and
Aid de Camp
United States
Volunteers.

Right.

" Entire devotion of heart to the
duty of the hour, is the
accomplishment of our work."

Rear.

Born in Salem
May 20, 1838,
Died at Brashear city,
Louisiana
June 2, 1863,
aged 25 years, 13 days.

Left.

" Blessed are the pure in heart
for they shall see God."

Lieut. Allen was son of J. F. and Lucy (Dodge) Allen, of Salem. He enlisted 27th of Oct., 1861, and on the same day, was authorized to raise thirty men for cavalry service, under Gen. Butler; commissioned as Lieut. of 1st

IX.

unattached company of cavalry, 20th of Feb., 1862; during the summer made 1st Lieut.,—and 29th of Sept. 1862, commenced duty as Aid de Camp on Gen. Weitzel's staff.

V.

Granite Monument, between Chapel Avenue and Anemone Path.

Joseph Peabody, son of Francis and Margaret (Knight) Peabody, of Middleton, born Aug. 12, 1757—lived in early life in Boxford and Middleton. At the commencement of the Revolution, he quit the occupation of an agriculturist, to participate in the more stirring scenes of a sea life on board of our private armed vessels where he distinguished himself as a brave and skilful officer. After the Revolution he commenced business as a ship owner and merchant at Salem. His enterprises in this department were rewarded with almost unprecedented success. He died Jan. 5, 1844.

VI.

Rustic Bridge.

Between the Main Entrance and the Superintendent's Lodge.

VII.

Marble Tablet, on Chapel Avenue.

R. S. Rogers and W. P. Endicott.

VIII.

On this Marble Monument, on Greenwood Avenue, is the following inscription :

William Harrison Prime
Hospital Steward U. S. A., born in
Charlestown Oct. 28, 1840,
died at Newbern, N. C.,
Sept. 2, 1864.
He loved and died for his country
in the Great Rebellion.

Why our earthly friend was taken
'Tis not ours to ask or say :
Father of the weary hearted,
Give us strength for this we pray.

IX.

Steatite Monument on Grove Avenue.

W. H. Foster.

X.

X.

Marble Monument, on Primrose Path.

C. M. Richardson.

Jonas
Richardson
eldest son of
Charles and Sarah
M. Richardson
Died
At Mobile Alabama
Sept. 10, 1839
aged 37 years.

XI.

Granite Monument, on Anemone Path.

Dudley Leavitt Pickman, son of William and Eliza (Leavitt) Pickman was born at Salem in 1779—died Nov. 4, 1846; a successful merchant, distinguished for his sound practical good sense and an inflexible regard to truth and justice.

XII.

J. H. Hanson.

Free-stone Tomb, surmounted by finely cut marble niche, covering statuette in bas-relief; built in 1853 on Highland Avenue.

XIII.

Marble Monument, on Hemlock Path.

S. W. Robertson.

XIV.

Granite Monument, with marble panels and shaft.
Erected in 1865, on Highland Avenue.

Benjamin Cox—born Sept. 8, 1779, d. Dec. 12, 1863.

XV.

Free-stone Monument, on Maple Avenue.

Nathan A. Frye.

XVI.

View in Viburnum Path.

XVII.

Moss Path from Geranium Path looking North.

XI.

XVIII.

Monument on Summit Avenue, corner of Jessamine Path.

HANNAH CROWNINSHIELD,
wife of Commodore
James Armstrong,
U. S. Navy
died May 4, 1834
aged 36 years.

ARMSTRONG.

XIX.

Double Tablet of Marble.

LEATHE.

Died in Hartford, Conn., Feb. 4, 1864 Rufus Augustus son of Levi T. and Maria P. Leathe, aged 25 years.	Died in Hartford, Conn., March 21, 1864 Susie Angeline daughter of Levi T. and Maria P. Leathe, aged 22 years.
Asleep in Jesus, Blessed Sleep,	From which none ever wake to weep.

4

XX.

Free-stone Monument, on Grove Avenue.

On the Front of Base inscribed

BRAZER.

Right side.

William Sever Brazer
a graduate of Harvard University
in the class of 1846,
and a member
of the second class
of the
U. S. Corps of Cadets,
in the year 1848-9.
Died at West Point,
17 July 1849
aged 22 years.

Left side.

In Testimony
of their respect for
the virtues
of their comrade,
and as a tribute
of regard
for his memory,
This Monument
is erected by
his classmates.

William S. Brazer was the son of Rev. John Brazer of the North Church, and was born in Salem, Sept. 9, 1826—graduated at Harvard in 1846, and immediately afterwards

BUFFORD'S LITH BOSTON.

XII.

entered the U. S. military academy at West Point, where he maintained a high stand and gave promise of future distinction in his profession. He was esteemed by his associates, a sincere and faithful friend, a high minded and honorable man.

XXI.

Sandstone Monument, on Aspen Path.

LEVERETT SALTONSTALL
born
June 13th, 1783
died May 8th, 1845.

Mary Elizabeth
wife of
Leverett Saltonstall
born March 1st 1788
died Jan. 11th 1858

SALTONSTALL

An open book in which is inscribed:

and heard a voice from heaven saying unto me write	Blessed are the dead which die in the Lord from henceforth. Blessed are the pure in heart for they shall see God.

Leverett Saltonstall was son of Nathaniel and Anna (White) Saltonstall of Haverhill, graduated at Harvard

College, 1802; studied law with Hon. W. Prescott of Salem; was eminent as an advocate, speaker of Mass. House of Representatives, President of Mass. Senate, first Mayor of Salem, Representative U. S. Congress, President of Bible Society of Salem and vicinity, President of Essex Agricultural Society, and of the Essex Bar, A. A. & S. H. S.—LL. D., Harvard, 1858, and a member of the Board of Overseers of Harvard College.

XXII.

View from the Cemetery Looking North.

XXIII.

Linden Avenue, Looking North.

XXIV.

Greenwood Avenue, Looking West.

XXV.

Lion and the Lamb.

Near the Main Entrance, at Junction of Highland and Cottage Avenues.

S. W. ROBERTSON.
J. H. BUFFORD & CO'S LITH. BOSTON.

XXVI.

Marble Monument, at Junction of Amaranth and Rue Paths.

The following inscriptions:

Front.

Wm. Bentley S. T. D.
born at Boston
June 22, 1759
ordained
Sept. 24, 1783;
died
Dec. 29, 1819

Right

Erected by the Second
Religious Society
in Salem.
In memory of
their
Minister.

Left.

The Rational
Christian,
Faithful Pastor,
Ardent Patriot,
and learned
Scholar,

XXVII.

In this enclosure, situated on Anemone Path, are several Monuments of marble, two of which are deserving of special notice.

1st—has the following inscription, written by Rev. James Flint, of Salem:

REV. TIMOTHY FLINT
whose writings have
won for him deserved
celebrity, was born in Reading Mass.
in 1780 where he died, on a visit from
the South Aug. 16, 1840,
aged 60.

—

He painted on his glowing page
The peerless valley of the west,
That shall to every coming age
His genius and his toils attest.
But wouldst thou, Gentle Pilgrim, know
What worth, what love endear'd the man,
This the lone hearts, that miss him, show
Better than storied marble can.

—

Rev. T. F., was the 4th son of William and Martha (Kimball) Flint, born in North Reading, July 23, 1780—graduated at Harvard College in 1800—ordained at Lunenburg, Nov. 30, 1802—dismissed at his own request, June 19, 1814, for the purpose of emigrating to the West.

COX
J.H. BUFFORD'S LITH. BOSTON.

2d—has inscribed the following:

James Flint, D. D.
died March 4, 1855,
aged 75 years.

Though long may seem the sad, slow years,
Till mourners with the mourned shall weep,
God then shall wipe away all tears,
And perfect love their bliss complete.

Rev. James Flint, sixth son of James and Mary (Hart) Flint, was born in North Reading Dec. 10, 1779—graduated at Harvard College in 1802—ordained in East Bridgewater 29th of Oct., 1806—installed at Salem, 19th of Sept., 1821, died at Salem, March 4, 1855. Married Lydia Harriet Deblois, and had nine children.

XXVIII.

Meadow Avenue, from the Danvers Entrance.

XXIX.

View from the Shreve Monument, Westward.

XXX.

View from the Cemetery, Looking West.

XXXI.

Meadow Avenue, Looking West.

XXXII.

Receiving Tomb.

Located on Highland Avenue.

XV.

LIST OF PROPRIETORS.

Proprietors.	Avenue.	Lot No.
Allen, J. Fiske,	Sylvan	37
Andrew, J. F., C. F. & I. W.,	Grove	73
Averill, Dolly and Susan,	Gentian	76
Arnold, Edward B.,	Anemone	102
Andrews, Joseph,	Grove	139
Annable, Nathaniel,	Sylvan	201
Andrews, N.,	Anemone	211
Abbott, Samuel E.,	Chapel	245
Archer, James,	Rosemary	246
Austin, Mrs. Elizabeth,	Valley	249
Andrews, Gilman,	Angelica	290
Archer, William,	Oak	302
Allice, John H.,	Eglantine	323
Archer, Mrs. Rebecca,	Halidon	398
Adams, Charles,	Magnolia	432
Adams, John G.,	Sassafras	479
Allen, George W.,	"	489
Archer, Augustus J.,	Highland	510
Allen, Ephraim,	Halidon	513
Ames, Mrs. Mary S.,	Jessamine	519
Austin, Eleazer,	Highland	524
Allen, Charles H.,	Daisy	542
Ashby, Sarah D.,	Ridge	565

Proprietors.	Avenue.	Lot No.
Allen, Bradstreet & Jos. P.,	Laurel	568
Allen, Mrs. Laura S.,	Maple	577
Austin, William,	Holly	586
Abbott, Philip,	"	587
Andrews, Hiram,	Anemone	590
Ashton, Wm. B.,	Ridge	593
Annable, Benj.,	Meadow	611
Ashton, F. P.,	Ridge	629
Agge, Jacob,	Cowslip	637
Allen, N. K.,	Angelica	647
Andrews, Charles & Robert,	Cowslip	687
Abbott, Daniel,	"	712
Armstrong, James	Summit	819
Ashby, Elias W.,	Broom	840
Adams, Nehemiah,	"	897
Arvedson, George,	Greenwood	919
Allen, David,	Broom	924
Abbott, Albert,	Greenwood	934
Allen, J. Fiske,	Beech	960
Ayres, Oliver,	"	967
Ayres, James,	"	1017
Adams, Chas. F.,	Holly	1059
Allen, Ira G.,	Forest	1076
Brown, James,	Anemone	12
Barry, Charles,	Grove	22
Browne, Benj. F.,	"	34
Brown, Wm. B.,	Rosemary	94

J.H. BUFDORD'S & SONS, LITH. BOSTON.

VIBURNUM AV.

XVI.

Proprietors.	Avenue.	Lot No.
Brazer, Rev. John,	Grove	95
Babbidge, Mrs. Nancy,	"	117
Battis, John H.,	Anemone	119
Briggs, Hepsibah,	Myrtle	127
Barton, Mary,	Chapel	137
Buffington, James	"	138
Briggs, Jas. B.,	Amaranth	143
Briggs, Wm.,	"	143
Brown, Mary, (Mrs. Gregory)	Grove	156
Berry, Aug.,	Primrose	170
Beckett, Jos.,	"	170
Batchelder, Andrew P.,	Sylvan	175
Batchelder, Oliver F.,	"	175
Barnard, Edward	Primrose	179
Bott ———	"	180
Barr, Rob't,	"	185
Bosson, Abraham,	Grove	198
Bailey, Geo.,	"	213
Berry, Jacob,	"	218
Berry, Geo. F.,	"	218
Boardman, Francis,	Columbine	233
Blaney, Wm.,	Rose	235
Burley, Susan,	Anemone	238
Burley, Elizabeth,	"	238
Burbank, E. A.,	Rosemary	246
Bailey, Mrs. Adeline D.,	Sylvan	280
Bryant, Timothy,	Summit	283

Proprietors.	Avenue.	Lot No.
Blaney, Philip,	Sylvan	298
Brown, Ephraim,	Gentian	307
Brown, Jonathan,	"	308
Brown, Geo. A.,	"	309
Brown, Jonathan,	"	311
Bedee, Appleton G.,	Summit	336
Buxton, Jos. Jr.,	Eglantine	353
Ballard, James,	Sylvan	355
Bennett, Chas. F.,	Halidon	357
Bennett, G. W.,	"	357
Bradford, Benj. W.,	Eglantine	367
Brown, Calvin,	Clematis	380
Brooks, Timothy,	Violet	387
Bullock, Isaac S.,	Halidon	419
Brooks, Luke, Jr.,	Summit	420
Brooks, Nath'l H.,	"	420
Batchelder, Richard,	Chestnut	439
Batchelder, Chas. M.,	"	440
Batchelder, Wm. L.,	"	441
Bowditch, D. C.,	Sassafras	467
Barker, Jos. W.,	Halidon	487
Brown, Epps,	Jessamine	502
Brown, Harvey,	"	503
Blake, Geo. F.,	Highland	504
Baldwin, Mrs. Ann,	"	518
Burke, Israel H.,	Sassafras	527
Batchelder, Samuel L.,	Maple	529

MOSS AV.

XVII.

Proprietors.	Avenue.	Lot No.
Bertram, John,	Grove	533
Barker, Thos.,	Violet	555
Brown, Samuel,	Maple	559
Brown, Geo. F.,	"	559
Brown, Samuel, Jr.,	"	559
Batchelder, David G.,	Highland	570
Buffum, Caleb,	Primrose	592
Burding, Henry W.,	Halidon	603
Butlind, John,	Yew	605
Bott, John C.,	Highland	608
Barnes, William,	Yew	610
Berry, Jacob W.,	Ridge	622
Batchelder, Wm. Jr.,	Cowslip	623
Burrill, George,	"	627
Brown, Willard H.,	Gentian	655
Battis, Joseph H.,	"	657
Blinn, John F.,	Yew	672
Berry, William H.,	Laurel	675
Brooks, William,	Holly	676
Bell, Mehitable C.,	Primrose	680
Bowditch Harriet	Gentian	692
Bowdoin, W. L.,	"	697
Batchelder, John H.,	Summit	703
Barlow, John,	"	707
Boyd, John,	Grove	715
Brown, Samuel,	Halidon	722
Burding, Elizabeth S.,	Angelica	725

Proprietors.	Avenue.	Lot No.
Browning, Geo. B.,	Angelica	730
Browne, J. V. & C. A.,	Halidon	726
Bryant, Hiram K.,	Violet	745
Beckett, D. C. & J. H..	Sassafras	752
Browne, A. G.,	Jessamine	755
Butman, F. C.,	Highland	760
Brown, Ephraim,	Gentian	763
Buxton, J. S., *et al.*,	Halidon	776
Brown, Eliz. H. & B. Howard,	Ridge	793
Baird, Martha,	"	801
Bassett, John B.,	"	806
Bowker, Mrs. L. R.,	Walnut	831
Blake, Samuel,	Ridge	832
Bell, John H.,	Halidon	837
Braden, James,	"	850
Buswell, Eben,	Ridge	898
Berry, Aaron W.,	Jessamine	899
Benson, Sam'l,	Woodbine	913
Bowditch, Geo ,	Forest	917
Bowdoin, D. W.,	Broom	922
Brown, J. W.,	Forest	933
Bruce, Geo. W.,	Greenwood	935
Buxton, Chas. H. & G. F.,	Beech	951
Buxton, Susan M.,	"	951
Brown, Lydia Ann,	Woodbine	972
Brookhouse, Robert,	Linden	994
Busteed, James,	Cypress	1015

XVIII.

J. H. BUFFORD & SONS' LITH. 313 WASH'N ST. BOSTON.

Proprietors.	Avenue.	Lot No.
Brown, Susan P.,	Beech	1017
Bomer, Caleb P.,	Woodbine	1031
Bray, Phebe,	"	1053
Beckford, A. N.,	Almond	1068
Brown, James M.,	Ridge	1081
Cleaveland, Wm.,	Columbine	9
Crocker & Morse,	Dell	13
Cabot, Jos. S.,	Chapel	23
Choate, Francis,	Magnolia	38
Chase, Geo. C.,	"	41
Carlton, Frazier,	Dell	43
Cole, Mrs. Sarah B.,	Grove	57
Cook, Henry,	Magnolia	83
Cook, John,	Grove	101
Colby, Samuel,	Gentian	110
Chaney, James,	Grove	116
Carlton, Jona. F.,	"	126
Collins, Deborah,	Myrtle	127
Currier, Edmund,	Valley	135
Chever, James W.,	Meadow	147
Cutts, Richard,	Grove	155
Cleaveland, Ebenezer,	"	156
Cook, William,	Primrose	169
Clark, J. D.,	Grove	172
Calef, John,	"	221
Churchill, Benj. H.,	Rosemary	251
Chipman, J. M.,	Anemone	252

Proprietors.	Avenue.	Lot No.
Caffrain, Wm. H.,	Sylvan	276
Carter, John,	Eglantine	289
Chapple, John D.,	Angelica	290
Collins, Hannah,	Summit	319
Cleaves, N. & J.,	Primrose	322
Clement, Henry,	Angelica	328
Conway, Chaplin,	Rosemary	348
Cummings, John,	Halidon	350
Chandler, Gardner L.,	Violet	360
Chandler, Luther,	Sylvan	363
Cook, Edward,	Clematis	381
Curran, Stephen,	Valley	395
Cox, Mrs. Sarah A.,	Highland	412
Carlton, Michael,	Willow	423
Cheever, Ira,	Highland	437
Campbell, J. G.,	"	448
Clough, Rob't P. & B P.,	Chestnut	456
Cook, James H.,	River	480
Colby, Hannah,	Sassafras	497
Cogswell, J. C.,	Halidon	499
Crowley, Wm.,	Aspen	512
Crowninshield, Ann,	Jessamine	520
Cory, Joseph W.,	"	536
Cox, Benjamin,	Highland	556
Clifford, Eben B.,	Ridge	565
Cook, Humphrey,	Holly	573
Culliton, John,	Highland	576

XIX.

Proprietors.	Avenue.	Lot No.
Chadwick, Henry G.,	Halidon	607
Cross, Joshua H.,	Yew	612
Creamer, Benjamin,	Highland	619
Creamer, Geo.,	"	620
Carlton, Edward F.,	Ridge	639
Clark, N. T.,	Violet	648
Crandall, C. A.,	Holly	671
Courtis, Deliverance,	Angelica	684
Chamberlain, Benj. P.,	Sassafras	689
Chamberlain, R. H.,	Spruce	699
Coker, John J.,	Holly	716
Coly, John,	"	728
Cochran, Joseph,	Jessamine	729
Clark, W. P.,	Hemlock	735
Cloutman, Joseph,	Primrose	762
Carleton, S. A.,	Cowslip	768
Curwen, Jas. B.,	Grove	798
Craig, Samuel,	Holly	812
Chapman, Geo. R.,	Highland	824
Conant, Herbert T.,	Halidon	836
Curtis, Emanuel,	Jessamine	838
Clark, John W.,	Ridge	855
Calley, Mary,	Highland	857
Cate, Wm.,	Laurel	864
Cutler, Harriet E.,	Halidon	865
Cobb, Seward P.,	Eglantine	870
Cabeen, Wm. & John,	Spruce	879

Proprietors.	Avenue.	Lot No.
Carlton, Oliver,	Sassafras	885
Chandler, Jos. D.,	Broom	886
Collins, Henry,	Forest	890
Cook, James,	"	910
Caulfield, A. D.,	Sassafras	930
Caulfield, James C.,	"	930
Crandall, Wm. H.,	Woodbine	950
Cook, James P.,	Greenwood	954
Cleveland, H. W. S.,	Halidon	959
Chandler, Jos. F.,	Beech	962
Cate, Shadrach M.,	Halidon	974
Cochrane, Wm.,	Woodbine	978
Converse, J. L.,	Ridge	1010
Carter, Eliz,	Forest	1028
Collins, Charles & Edward,	Beech	1044
Downing, Thomas,	Violet	5
Dodge, Pickering,	Barberry	36
Dexter, John,	Magnolia	66
Davis, H. G.,	Grove	103
Daly, James,	Gentian	184
Dodge, Thomas S.,	Anemone	189
Dodge, Eben,	Lupine	192
Donaldson, Alexander,	Gentian	207
Davis, Rodman J.,	"	216
Draper, William,	Sylvan	228
Dearborn, Chas. A.,	Rosemary	278

XX.

Proprietors.	Avenue.	Lot No.
Dowbridge, Andrew,	Willow	291
Dickson, Thomas,	Primrose	341
Dickson, Thomas Jr.,	"	342
Dickson, Augustus,	"	343
Daken, Timothy H.,	"	358
Davis, Wm. H.,	Halidon	383
Dodge, Luke E.,	"	389
Daniels, R. S. & D.,	Violet	399
Daland, Mrs. E. H.,	Highland	412
Davis, Jas. B.,	Chestnut	438
Dwyer, John,	Sassafras	447
Dodge, Pickering,	Columbine	474
Davis, Richard,	Violet	477
Davis, Warren P.,	Halidon	486
Draper, Jno. W.,	Grove	492
Dodge, Jos. S.,	Holly	506
Dexter, Naomi,	Daisy	534
Debaker, Victor F.,	Violet	537
Daland, Tucker,	Highland	563
Dwyer, Hannah,	Sassafras	598
Dale, Joseph,	Ridge	601
Dearborn, Henry C.,	Halidon	604
Dow, Edward A.,	Jessamine	609
Daniels, Wm.,	Ridge	618
Daniels, Stephen,	Violet	621
Dabney, J. P.,	Yew	643
Danforth, J. N. & J. K.,	Ridge	678

Proprietors.	Avenue.	Lot No.
Danforth, S. G., & E. F.	"	679
Dockham, Stephen B.,	Spruce	717
Dudley, Daniel C.,	Grove	734
Day, John,	Violet	751
Derby, Henry,	Spruce	753
Day, Eliz,	Ridge	801
Dawson, Geo.,	Laurel	802
Dwinell, I. A.,	Holly	859
Davis, Wm. B.	Halidon	871
Draper, Caroline S.,	Ridge	874
Dodge, Isaac B,.	Halidon	877
Davidson, John,	Halidon	881
Daniels, Blake,	Ridge	887
Dole, Wm. T.,	Highland	908
Davis, Jacob P.,	Forest	918
Dean, Geo.,	Ridge	945
Dole, Lydia A ,	Laurel	955
Dalrymple, James,	Greenwood	975
Dalrymple, Simon O.,	"	976
Daland, Joanna & Mary E.	Forest	982
Deland, Helen M.,	Beech	1026
Dole, Moses T. & Charles A.,	Linden	1029
Dane, Joseph F.,	Beech	1052
Emmerton, Ephraim,	Anemone	131
Evans, Cornelius,	Grove	136
Endicott, Wm. P.,	Chapel	153

XXI.

Proprietors.	Avenue.	Lot No.
Eagleston, John H.,	Columbine	191
Eustis, E. S.,	Anemone	211
Everett, L S.,	Columbine	220
Emerson, Brown,	Oak	392
Eddy, Rev. D. C.,	Valley	403
Eastman, M. H.,	Chestnut	444
Eustis, Nancy R. & Betsy,	Laurel	635
Elwell, Chas. B.,	Spruce	788
Emerson, Geo. F.,	Forest	1018
Frost, Caleb S.,	Columbine	7
Flint, James,	Anemone	21
Foster, Josiah,	Dell	27
Farnham, Jona. M.,	"	71
Fairfield, Margaret,	Anemone	33
Frothingham, Joseph,	Amaranth	46
Felt, John G.,	Amaranth	74
Felt, Nath'l H.,	Valley	80
Felton, Wm. T.,	"	115
Felt, J. P.,	Hemlock	151
Foster, Wm. H.	Dell	194
Farnham, P. I.,	Columbine	209
Foote, Caleb,	Chapel	212
Farnham, Nathan,	Grove	234
Felton, John S.,	Magnolia	264
Foster, Gideon,	"	271
Fuller, Samuel T. & R. H.,	Summit	324

Proprietors.	Avenue.	Lot No.
Farnum, Joseph,	Oak	334
Fogg, Julian A.,	Primrose	344
Fisk, John B.,	Highland	393
Floyd, S. P.,	Angelica	397
Florence, Thomas J.,	Violet	368
Fowler, Joseph,	Chestnut	408
Fabens, Benjamin,	Valley	428
Felt, Benjamin Jr.,	Violet	454
Friend, Joel,	Amaranth	461
Felton, Jonathan M.,	Halidon	491
Farnham, C. B. & Henry,	Daisy	538
Ferguson, Samuel,	"	546
Frye, Nathaniel,	Maple	566
Farrington, Geo. P.,	"	600
Foulklin, Geo.,	Laurel	606
Fisher, Thorpe,	Gentian	655
Frye, Joseph,	Maple	664
Foster, Joseph G.,	Ridge	670
Farley, G. G.,	Holly	676
Fletcher, Rodney C.,	Gentian	700
Frye, Daniel,	Grove	718
Fowler, Geo.,	Holly	766
Fernald, Giles C.,	Ridge	771
Fuller, Enoch P.,	Hemlock	780
Forness, Joseph W.,	Highland	786
Fountain, Nancy A.,	Broom	845
Fitz, Josiah,	Laurel	854

BUFFORDS' LITH. BOSTON.

VIEW FROM THE CEMETERY LOOKING NORTH.

XXII.

Proprietors.	Avenue.	Lot No.
Fisk, Phocius,	Halidon,	860
Fernald, Stephen,	Laurel	864
Flint, Simeon,	"	866
Fogg, Sylvester, and Heirs,	Greenwood	888
Fellows, Israel,	Halidon	893
Felt, John V.,	Forest	914
Ferguson, Edward A.,	Beech	966
Felt, Ephraim and Catharine,	"	977
Fairfield, James,	Cypress	1001
Fuller, Edward,	Ridge	1004
Floyd, Reuben H.,	Holly	1011
Fanning, James,	Cypress	1016
Fisk, Joseph E.,	Woodbine	1032
Farley, James H.,	"	1060
Fabens, Benjamin F.,	Greenwood	1079
Gardner, Wm. F.,	Valley	31
Goodhue, James B.,	Grove	35
Goodhue, Abner,	Magnolia	39
Grant, Henry,	Gentian	75
Goodwin, John,	Grove	219
Gould, Charles P.,	"	232
Goldsmith, Nancy,	Valley,	262
Green, James,	Highland	282
Gardner, Albert S.,	Grove	286
Gordon, Hiram E.,	Eglantine	295
Goss, Richard,	Eglantine	297

Proprietors.	Avenue.	Lot No
Gardner, Henry,	Dell	331
Goss, Ezekiel,	Angelica	335
Gardner, Joseph 3d,	Primrose	338
Goodridge, John W.,	Summit	340
Goodell, Abner C.,	Halidon	347
Gomes, Joseph,	Chapel	402
Goodwin, Thomas,	Chestnut	410
Gordon, M. A., Chas., & O. A.,	Highland	414
Graves, William B.,	Angelica	415
Goldthwait, Moses,	Oak	417
Gardner, Charles,	Highland	448
Grant, Fanny,	Summit	465
Griffen, Eben,	Highland	485
Goldthwait, Aaron,	Sassafras	490
Gardner, John,	Halidon	493
Goldthwait, Willard,	Jessamine	507
Gifford, Thomas J.,	Violet	515
Gifford, James B.,	"	516
Gifford, Rufus B.,	"	517
Goodwin, Mrs. E. C.,	Jessamine	522
Goodhue, Nathaniel,	Gentian	535
Goldthwait, J. A.,	Maple	585
Goodhue, Catharine,	Summit	651
Goldthwait, Elizabeth P.,	Laurel	682
Gardner, Daniel B.,	Violet	690
Goldthwait, Aaron,	Holly	691
Glover, Joseph E.,	Halidon	723

BUFFORD & SONS LITH. BOSTON.

LINDEN AV.

Proprietors.	Avenue.	Lot No.
Gardner, Samuel,	Hemlock	742
Goldthwait, William J.,	"	744
Gillan, John,	Ridge	772
Gwinn, T. W. & J. S.,	Halidon	774
Griffen, Nathaniel,	Grove	821
Grant, John,	Laurel	842
Getchell, J. & B. W.,	Hemlock,	847
Gray, Wm. B.,	Broom	848
Glover, George D.,	Spruce	878
Gardner, Elizabeth, Est. of	Halidon	905
Gray, Benjamin A.,	Spruce	920
Grover, John,	Halidon	936
Gibney, John,	Greenwood	949
Goss, Francis,	Spruce	964
Gordon, Rufus L.,	Woodbine	973
Goldsmith, John H.,	Beech	1030
Gardner, Stephen W.,	Forest	1034
Govea, Augustus E. B.,	Beech	1035
Greenough, John W.,	Spruce	1043
Hill, William & Richard,	Meadow	2
Harrington, Jonas,	Gentian	28
Hanson, Elijah A.,	Amaranth	29
Hubbard, Oliver,	Dell	65
Haskell, E. & D. C.,	Rose	78
Hodgdon, Samuel & G. C.,	Meadow	88
Harrington, L. B.,	Valley	91

Proprietors.	Avenue.	Lot No
Hunt, Thomas,	Grove	101
Hoyt, Erastus,	"	104
Huse, John,	Valley	112
Hill, William,	Aster	123
Haley, Shillaber,	Grove	136
Hall, Eliphalet,	Grove	152
Harris, James,	Primrose	186
Howard, Charles G.,	Gentian,	187
Howe, Israel T.,	Primrose	208
Hubon, Henry G.,	Columbine	223
Houghton, Lucy A. D.,	Sumach	237
Howes, F.,	Anemone	238
Holmes, Thomas,	Valley	259
Henfield Division S. of T.	Angelica	269
Haskell, Miss Eliza,	Oak	281
Hood, Jacob,	Highland	294
Holman, Lyman,	Angelica	326
Harrington, Chas. & Aug.,	Rosemary	333
Haines, John K.,	Eglantine	339
Hurd, Randall F.,	Halidon	349
Hooper, Nathaniel,	"	351
Hazelton, John,	Grove	361
Harris, Eliza B.,	Amaranth	366
Healy, Mrs. Mary,	Halidon	372
Higbee, Lemuel,	Violet	376
Harris, George O.,	Halidon	384
Hammond, John,	"	404

GREENWOOD AV.

XXIV

Proprietors.	Avenue.	Lot No.
Higbee, Charles,	Halidon,	409
Hoyt, Robert,	Chestnut	410
Hunt, Joseph,	Highland	426
Harris, N. B.,	Highland	426
Haskell, Jacob,	Chestnut	443
Haskins, Susan L.,	Halidon	445
Hazelton, Phebe W.,	Myrtle	457
Hodgdon, George C.,	Valley	458
Hodges, Gamaliel,	Halidon	471
Harron, William M.,	"	498
Hurd, Charles,	Jessamine	500
Hiltz, Jacob,	Halidon	540
Hanson, Joseph H.,	Highland	549
Hutchinson, George C.,	Ridge	571
Hill, Increase S.,	Jessamine	613
Hammond, Eliza S.,	Ridge	617
Hodgkins, Nathaniel R.,	Sylvan	625
Hart, John,	Willow	640
Horton, Charles E.,	Gentian	646
Hunt, William,	Jessamine	658
Hayman, John & Phebe,	Broom	665
Henderson, Daniel,	Holly	686
Howes, William B.,	Grove	704
Haskell, Elijah,	Angelica	711
Hobbs, Horatio,	Grove	739
Haraden, Abigail,	Summit	754
Hill, Samuel,	Ridge	765

Proprietors.	Avenue.	Lot No.
Hanson, G. H. A., *et al.*,	Halidon	776
Hall, David,	Holly	777
Hawley, Robert,	"	777
Hill, Henry B.,	Yew	779
Hildreth, Elbridge H.,	Highland	805
Hanson, Sarah,	Hemlock	818
Haskell, Mark,	Ridge	849
Heard, Mary C.,	Ridge	849
Hamilton, Mary,	Laurel	852
Honeycomb, W. H. & T. P.,	Spruce	876
Hazelton, Augustus,	Cowslip	902
Hadley, Willis, & George S.,	Forest	912
Horton, Nathaniel,	"	914
Harrington, Richard,	Greenwood	915
Hall, William H.,	Woodbine	942
Hodges, George A.,	Halidon	952
Hunt, Thomas,	Greenwood	958
Hooper, Edward,	Beech	967
Herrick, Isaac,	Woodbine	980
Hayward, Cyrus L.,	"	981
Hall, William H.,	"	986
Hadley, Thomas D.,	Forest	988
Haskell, Daniel,	Cypress	999
Haskell, Jacob S.,	"	1000
Hill, Increase S.,	Jessamine	1005
Hoffman, Charles,	Greenwood	1013
Howard, Betsey,	Ridge	1033

Buffords' Lith. Boston.

XXV.

Proprietors.	Avenue.	Lot No.
Hood, David,	Beech	1048
Hoyt, Stephen,	Mulberry	1074
Hatch, Lemuel B.,	"	1077
Innis, John A.,	Rose	111
Ingalls, Collins,	Primrose	186
Ives, William, and S. B.,	Magnolia	202
Ireland, Isaac M.,	Grove	257
Ingersoll, Margaret,	Willow	423
Joseph, Richard C.,	Meadow	14
Johnson, Samuel,	Anemone	16
Jacobs, Warren M.,	Sylvan	61
Jacobs, George,	Rose	90
Jeanes, Joseph,	Grove	241
Johnson, Emery, Trustees of,	Columbine	270
Jackson, William E.,	Eglantine	296
Jackson, Jacob S.,	"	318
Johnson, Thomas M.,	Violet	354
Jones, John F.,	Angelica	397
Jewett, John,	Violet	453
Jenks, Lydia,	Summit	460
Johnson, Nathaniel,	Highland	504
Johnson, S. S.,	Jessamine	505
Jewett, Thomas S.,	Maple	530
Judkins, Edward H.,	Daisy	546
Jewett, D. H.,	Halidon	547

Proprietors.	Avenue.	Lot No.
Julio, William T.,	Highland	550
Jones, Samuel G.,	Halidon	572
Jewett, Moses,	Jessamine	626
Jackson, Andrew & Ellen L.,	Violet	652
Jenks, Henry E.,	Summit	760
Jackson, Benjamin,	Pine	789
Jackman, Nathaniel C.,	Woodbine	990
Jewett, G. B.,	Halidon	995
Johnson, Thomas M.,	Cypress	1002
Johnson, Thomas H.,	"	1003
Jeffrey, John,	Forest	1007
Jelly, Samuel,	Beech	1036
Jackson, John,	Mulberry	1066
Jackson, William H.,	Greenwood	1075
Kennedy, Samuel,	Dell	30
Kenny, John,	Gentian	79
Kimball, Mark,	Valley	84
Kimball, Abraham,	"	133
King, James, B.,	Grove	144
Kenny, Jonathan A.,	Sumach	173
Kimball, James S ,	Gentian	203
Kenny, William,	Grove	222
Kinsman, N. Jr.,	"	242
Kezer, Albert,	Chapel	268
Kimball, Nathaniel,	Eglantine	288
Knight, Thorndike F.,	Angelica	327

XXVI

Proprietors.	Avenue.	Lot No.
Knowlton, Sarah,	Oak	334
Kimball, William,	Gentian	250
Kimball, E. D., E. G., & N. A.,	Violet	352
Knight, John,	Halidon	369
Knight, Albert,	Aster	379
Kimball, James,	Maple	560
Kimball, Eben D.,	"	683
Kyle, Robert,	Cowslip	731
Kelley, Mary,	Holly	741
Keating, Mary,	Maple	747
Kenny, Jonathan, Heirs of	Pine	749
Kenny, George W.,	"	749
Kimball, Hannah W.,	Hemlock	750
Kelly, Nathaniel,	Jessamine	775
Kimball, Mark,	Violet	826
Kinsman, N. J.,	Beech	943
Kimball, Edward,	Linden	1008
Kimball, Jessie M.,	"	1008
Kimball, Elbridge G.,	"	1008
Kenny, Jonathan A.,	Yew	1024
Lefavor, Joseph,	Magnolia	3
Lamson, Asa Jr.,	Gentian	11
Lee, John C.,	Chapel	26
Lowe, Caleb,	Magnolia	69
Low, A. T.,	Grove	155
Lampher, Judith,	Primrose	164

Proprietors.	Avenue.	Lot No.
Lane, Edward B.,	Gentian	204
Leavitt, J. S. & Est. of O.,	Primrose	206
Long, Isaac C.,	Columbine	220
Long, Isaac C.,	"	224
Luscomb, Henry,	Grove	257
Lord, James & Michael,	Sylvan	260
Lummus, Ezra,	Grove	292
Lander, William W.,	Summit	304
Louvrier, Estate of P. C.,	Oak	305
Lang, Benjamin,	Violet	373
Looby, Thomas,	Highland	405
Lawrence, George,	Magnolia	442
Lovejoy, John,	Sassafras	472
Lewis, Thomas R.,	"	488
Lord, Lucy,	Angelica	501
Lendholm, Frederick,	Ridge	548
Lowd, Mark,	Yew	616
Lord, Daniel B.,	Holly	668
Leach, Eliza N.,	Spruce	695
Low, Hannah,	Chestnut	710
Lee, Isaac,	Hemlock	736
Lambert, Laura L.,	Chestnut	799
Lassen, Peter,	Pine	810
Lefavor, John,	Sassafras	820
Luscomb, J. W.,	Ridge	869
Lander, William A.,	Beech	965
Lamson, William,	"	969

XXVII.

Proprietors.	Avenue.	Lot No.
Lewis, Samuel,	Woodbine	970
Lord, Nathaniel J.,	Tulip	987
Lefavor, J. W.,	Woodbine	991
Lord, William N.,	Linden	1022
Lambert, Porter,	Beech	1025
Leavitt, Israel P.,	Laurel	1080
Morse & Crocker.	Dell	13
Merritt, David,	Cowslip	20
Merrill, Benjamin,	Chapel	52
Melcher, Edward,	Grove	56
Mugford, Charles D.,	Anemone	85
Munroe, George,	Primrose	154
Morse, John & N. P.,	Grove	158
Madison, John,	Valley	174
Munroe, George,	Primrose	181
Meade, William J.,	Grove	213
Mills, L. & S.,	"	243
McCloy, Alexander,	Gentian	256
Mackie, John,	Valley	266
Marston, Susan,	Gentian	273
McKenzie, W. H.,	Eglantine	374
McKenzie, R. A.,	"	375
Millett, Charles,	Violet	388
Murphy, John,	Clematis	394
Mack, Elisha,	Amaranth	427
Messer, Phebe,	Gentian	431

Proprietors.	Avenue.	Lot No.
Moody, Moses B.,	Dell	434
May, Joshua,	Sassafras	449
Mellus, Henry,	Halidon	450
Mann, Sarah B.,	"	455
Morse, Francis W.,	Jessamine	514
Miller, James,	Violet	528
Mahoney, Jeremiah,	"	537
Magoon, Thomas,	Daisy	541
Merrill, Franklin A.,	Columbine	558
McKey, John,	Jessamine	569
Moreland, G. W. & John H.,	Laurel	580
Murphy, James,	Eglantine	599
Mansfield, Lucretia,	Yew	615
Merrill, M. S.,	Sylvan	625
Manning, Charles H.,	Violet	653
Morse, Lucius B.,	Cowslip	663
Millett, Joseph H.,	Summit	685
Mullet, George W.,	Laurel	758
Moulton, Frederick,	Holly	766
Marston, Daniel,	Violet	781
Morse, Eben H.,	Ridge	791
Muhlig, Robert,	Jessamine	796
Marshall, Joseph,	Hemlock	800
Morse, Benjamin,	Violet	803
Morse, William H.,	Holly	811
Manning, Daniel H.,	"	811
Mackintire, John,	Holly	812

Proprietors.	Avenue.	Lot No
Manning, William S.,	Holly	827
Martin, C. W., Estate of,	Halidon	835
Morse, Eleazer H.,	Ridge	839
Mansfield, Ira,	Laurel	863
Messervy, William S.,	Greenwood	883
Manning, D. C.,	Forest	904
Millett, Nathan,	Beech	906
Mansfield, Daniel H.,	Greenwood	907
Matthews, Richard,	Spruce	932
Moore, Charles E.,	Holly	948
Masury, Samuel,	Beech	956
Masury, John,	Beech	956
Morris, Joseph,	Spruce	963
Mansfield, N. B.,	Linden	971
Muchmore, Richard,	Cypress	985
Marshall, David,	Cypress	999
Mayer, Joseph,	Greenwood	1041
Maloon, William,	Beech	1051
McCousland, George A.,	Almond	1069
Miller, William,	Forest	1073
Newhall, G. G.,	Sumach	48
Nichols, Thomas,	Valley	113
Noah, Samuel,	"	114
Nichols, William F.,	Chapel	138
Newhall, Joseph,	Sumach	173
Needham, Ezekiel,	Grove	254

Proprietors.	Avenue.	Lot No.
Needham, Lydia,	Grove	254
Needham, Daniel,	"	254
Nichols, John R.,	Gentian	310
Nutting, William G.,	Eglantine	315
Newhall, William H.,	Halidon	356
Noble, James,	Aster	379
Norfolk, E. L.,	Angelica	396
Norfolk, Joseph & J. R.,	"	397
Nay, Joshua,	Sassafras	449
Neal, Joseph,	Jessamine	495
Noyes, Enoch K.,	Halidon	523
Newton, John H.,	Highland	595
Needham, Thomas,	Laurel	635
Nichols, Thomas J.,	Gentian	654
Nichols, Mary F.,	Halidon	659
Neal, David A.,	Sassafras	662
Nelson, William H.,	Hemlock	738
Nichols, David,	Violet	743
Nourse, Ebenezer,	Holly	778
Newcomb, C. & C. H.,	Holly	783
Noyes, Isaac S.,	Ridge	814
Nason, David,	Halidon	843
Nichols, William H.,	Ridge	875
Nichols, L. B.,	Woodbine	992
Nichols, Nathan,	Greenwood	1065
Osborne, Stephen,	Chapel	67

MEADOW AV. FROM THE DANVERS ENTRANCE.

XXVIII.

Proprietors.	Avenue.	Lot No.
Osborn, Sylvester & A. K.,	Myrtle	99
O'Donnell, Mrs. Mary,	Anemone	100
Osborne, William Henry,	Meadow	145
Osborne, George A.,	Moss	197
Ober, Andrew,	Willow	236
Osborn, Sylvester,	Myrtle	265
Ottignon, Firman,	Halidon	390
Osgood, Thaddeus,	Valley	395
Oliver, W. F. & Eliza,	Jessamine	500
Osborn, Dennison W.,	Columbine	557
Osgood, Mary E.,	Laurel	578
Osborne, Ezra,	Chestnut	713
Osborne, G. F., W. P., & S.,	Maple	834
Osgood, John C.,	Halidon	891
Osgood, Elizabeth C.,	"	931
Odell, William H.,	Laurel	938
Osborne, Henry M.,	Woodbine	993
Osborne, George,	Tulip	1012
Odlin, Mary,	Holly	1061
Page, Jeremiah,	Anemone	8
Putnam, Jacob,	Highland	18
Payson, E. H.,	Magnolia	42
Peabody, Joseph,	Chapel	49
Peabody, Francis,	Anemone	50
Peabody, George,	"	51
Peirson, Abel L.,	Rosemary	54

Proprietors.	Avenue.	Lot N o
Poor, William,	Sylvan	58
Poole, Fitch,	"	59
Poole, Leonard,	"	60
Phelps, Sylvester,	Meadow	89
Pitman, Samuel,	Valley	93
Peirce, Jonathan,	Anemone	96
Putnam, David,	Gentian	106
Peabody, David R ,	Clematis	107
Putnam, Perley,	Gentian	109
Putnam, Allen,	Chapel	120
Phelps, William & William Jr.,	Rose	128
Peele, J. Willard,	Meadow	149
Phillips Stephen C.,	Amaranth	150
Peabody, Oliver,	Grove	171
Pope, Lott,	"	177
Prime, Thomas H.,	Anemone	183
Plander, John G.,	"	190
Pulsifer, D. & J.,	Dell	199
Parker, William B.,	Grove	215
Peabody, Harriet F.,	Rosemary	227
Pike, William B.,	Highland	240
Pratt, William,	Willow	244
Peirce, John B.,	Gentian	247
Pope, W. H.,	"	256
Preston, Jonathan,	Grove	261
Palfray, Edward,	Primrose	274
Perkins, Jos., Daniel, & A. S.,	Moss	293

Proprietors.	Avenue.	Lot No.
Palmer, Charles,	Eglantine	301
Pickman, D. L.,	Anemone	303
Palfrey, B. C., M. C., & T.,	Gentian	312
Perkins, Jonathan W.,	Eglantine	316
Pray, Isaac C.,	Summit	320
Patterson, Eliphalet S.,	Summit	324
Potter, Mrs. Lydia,	Rue	345
Perkins, J. S. & Aaron,	Violet	359
Putnam, Amos P.,	Chapel	401
Putnam, Mrs. S.,	Highland	412
Parker, J. Brooks,	Chestnut	421
Palmer, Mrs. Mary P.,	Gentian	430
Patterson, Nancy,	Grove	433
Prince, Elizabeth,	Sassafras	446
Phipps, Samuel & Samuel Jr.,	Halidon	466
Plumer, W. G.,	"	468
Putnam, Joseph W.,	Sassafras	475
Palmer, W. H. & Theron,	Angelica	476
Peirce, David,	Jessamine	508
Pray, Daniel H.,	"	509
Pope, Eleazer & Lucy E.,	Ridge	511
Potter, Mrs. S. C.,	Jessamine	521
Patterson, Benjamin,	Daisy	539
Peirce, George C.,	"	544
Price, George,	"	544
Price, William H. & John Jr.,	"	545
Pratt, John,	Holly	567

Proprietors.	Avenue.	Lot No.
Porter, Ann,	Sylvan	624
Pease, Richard,	Jessamine	630
Price, Charles,	"	630
Pearson, Nathan,	Highland	636
Pinkham, Mrs. Lydia,	Sassafras	644
Perley, John,	Violet	649
Perkins, John,	"	650
Prince, John,	Holly	668
Putnam, James H.,	"	671
Phipps, Joseph,	"	681
Perley, Jonathan,	Angelica	701
Perley, Jonathan Jr.,	"	701
Paine, Joseph A.,	Holly	709
Parsons, Mary,	"	714
Price, Eben N.,	Angelica	720
Pousland, Abigail D.,	Highland	733
Perry, J. W.,	Primrose	762
Prescott, Susan,	Primrose	762
Peabody, George, (London)	Locust	767
Prescott, William J.,	Laurel	773
Parsons, Frederick Jr.,	Jessamine	775
Poole, W., Estate of,	Highland	785
Phippen, Benjamin,	Holly	787
Perry, Benjamin,	Sassafras	808
Putnam, Nathan,	Holly	817
Potter, Joseph,	Grove	822
Pingree, Anna,	Halidon	828

BUFFORD'S LITH. BOSTON.

VIEW FROM THE SHREVE MONUMENT.

XXIX.

Proprietors.	Avenue.	Lot No.
Poole, Ward, Estate of,	Highland	830
Putnam, Francis,	Laurel	853
Pratt, Elisha,	Holly	859
Phelps, William,	Broom	868
Punchard, John P.,	Halidon	871
Peabody, Alfred,	Greenwood	884
Pitman, Samuel Jr.,	"	892
Peirce, Mrs. Caroline,	Halidon	894
Phippen, Robert A.,	Cowslip	901
Pinel, Philip P.,	Spruce	903
Peabody, George, (London)	Locust	909
Pitman, Nathaniel,	Forest	911
Parsons, John H.,	"	923
Parsons, Mrs. Betsey,	"	937
Pingree, David,	Greenwood	953
Patch, I. J., I. H., & W. H. H.,	Forest	989
Punchard, George,	Halidon	995
Peirce, C. H.,	Woodbine	996
Perkins, Emery J.,	Cypress	998
Pingree, S. R.,	Woodbine	1014
Pitman, Nathaniel,	Forest	1019
Pratt, William,	"	1019
Potter, George A.,	Greenwood	1042
Perkins, David,	Beech	1046
Prime, Thomas H.,	Greenwood	1047
Patterson, Nicholas,	Forest	1050
Pindar, John,	Woodbine	1054

Proprietors.	Avenue.	Lot No.
Perkins, Elijah R.,	Yew	1055
Pickering, John F.,	Ridge	1062
Phippen, Joseph H.,	Sassafras	1067
Perkins, Edward B.,	Ridge	1070
Pratt, Leonard,	Beech	1087
Pease, George W.,	Cypress	1098
Richardson, Eunice,	Anemone	17
Reed, Benjamin,	Magnolia	19
Rose, Harriet,	Chapel	25
Richardson, Charles M.,	Dell	44
Ropes, Timothy,	Amaranth	47
Rupp, Andrew,	Anemone	64
Rideout, Nathaniel,	Gentian	72
Rogers, Nathaniel L.,	Chapel	81
Rider, Joseph,	Meadow	87
Robbins, Thomas,	Rose	90
Ross, Joseph & Nathaniel,	Anemone	98
Ross, David,	Valley	108
Robinson, John,	Anemone	121
Rugg, Ann M.,	Grove	124
Ropes, Joseph,	"	125
Reed, John,	Meadow	148
Rogers, R. S.,	Chapel	153
Redmond, Edward,	Magnolia	163
Richards, Lewis D.,	Willow	244
Russell, H. J. & G. W.,	Anemone	252

Proprietors.	Avenue.	Lot No
Richardson, Charles,	Primrose	255
Roberts, David,	Grove	272
Ruee, James T.,	Rosemary	300
Richardson, W. H.,	Eglantine	301
Richardson, James,	"	313
Rutherford, Oliver,	Myrtle	362
Ropes, Henry,	Halidon	424
Ropes, John T.,	Sassafras	467
Roberts, John,	"	478
Rose, Joseph Jr.,	River	484
Russell, William,	Cedar	494
Rupp, Frederick,	Daisy	551
Rowell, Edward,	Holly	588
Ropes, William & Hardy,	Ridge	597
Reynolds, Moses C.,	Highland	633
Remond, John,	Ridge	666
Radford, Charles F. & Benj.,	Yew	672
Radford, John,	Yew	672
Rust, F. A. P. & Benjamin,	Holly	674
Randall, Mrs. Samuel,	Columbine	696
Russell, Henry,	Violet	740
Robertson, Stratton W.,	Hemlock	784
Ropes, R. W. & Co.,	Laurel	792
Ramsdell, Margaret,	Holly	797
Reith, John & John Jr.,	Jessamine	823
Ruee, Philip B. & H. A.,	Cedar	825
Roundy, Charles,	Halidon	861

Proprietors.	Avenue.	Lot No
Rogers, J. W.,	Eglantine	867
Roundy, Thomas Jr.,	Forest	890
Ropes, George & Joseph Aug.,	Jessamine	928
Rocko, Matthew M.,	Beech	947
Ross, Julian A.,	Holly	968
Roome, William,	Yew	1049
Roberts, David,	Ridge	1063
Robinson, John G.,	Broom	1091
Saunders, Robert S.,	Grove	1
Stickney, M. A.,,	"	4
Sutton, William,	Sylvan	62
Stimpson, J. C.,	Anemone	63
Southwick, P. R.,	Magnolia	66
Sprague, Joseph G.,	"	83
Stanley, Edward,	Anemone	105
Southward, Thomas W.,	"	119
Silsbee, Nathaniel,	Amaranth	129
Silsbee, N. Jr.,	"	130
Sargent, Winthrop,	Valley	134
Sprague, Joseph E.,	Grove	140
Shepard, Michael,	Dell	142
Swasey, John,	Primrose	161
Stickney, Richard,	"	161
Stoddard, Benjamin,	"	165
Stoddard, Daniel,	"	166
Smith, Jesse Jr.,	Valley	168

BUFFORD'S LITH. BOSTON.

VIEW FROM THE CEMETERY, LOOKING WEST.

XXX.

Proprietors.	Avenue.	Lot No.
Smith, William E.,	Gentian	187
Safford, Samuel A.,	Amaranth	193
Southwick, Joseph,	Gentian	195
Smith, Caleb,	Moss	196
Slocum, Ebenezer,	Primrose	208
Saunders, William,	Grove	210
Shreve, Mary,	"	221
Shreve, Benjamin & Maria,	"	221
Silsbee, Zach. F.,	Amaranth	225
Silsbee, B. H. & J. H.,	"	226
Sheldon, Elizabeth,	Willow	244
Seaver, Mrs. Rachel,	Primrose	275
Searle, Nathaniel,	Highland	284
Symonds, Mrs. Eliza G.,	Oak	299
Skinner, M. L.,	Highland	306
Shillaber, Jona., Jas., D., & Eliz.,	Eglantine	313
Smith, James A.,	Angelica	329
Smith, William C.,	"	330
Stone, Thomas F.,	Primrose	332
Spaulding, Levi,	Magnolia	337
Stevens, James F.,	Oak	346
Staniford, Charles,	Willow	386
Shillaber, Eben, *et al.*,	Violet	399
Southwick, Geo. W.,	Angelica	416
Symonds, Charles A.,	Highland	418
Symonds, Thomas,	Violet	451
Saunders, David E.,	"	452

Proprietors.	Avenue.	Lot No.
Stiles, Dean,	Chestnut	459
Shepard, J. B. & S. D.,	Halidon	462
Shepard, Isaac B.,	Sassafras	464
Skinner, Richard,	"	469
Segee, Mary H.,	Cedar	470
Smith, William B.,	Angelica	476
Swett, Sarah M.,	Halidon	540
Saunders, Thomas M.,	Daisy	543
Strout, Eben B.,	Highland	554
Sims, Richard H.,	Maple	561
Stevens, Ephraim,	Columbine	562
Story, Augustus,	Halidon	564
Shepard, I. D.,	Angelica	574
Short, Lydia T.,	Holly	575
Symonds, Charles W.,	Laurel	579
Snell, Nicholas T.,	Jessamine	582
Smith, C. A. & H. W.,	"	583
Savory, Benjamin,	Maple	584
Sanger, George F.,	Highland	632
Stanley, M. A ,	Willow	640
Stafford, William M.,	"	642
Sewall, Charles C.,	Oak	645
Smith, James F.,	Cowslip	660
Smith, Sarah L.,	Ridge	667
Smith, Joseph A.,	Ridge,	670
Seccomb, Eben,	Highland	688
Southward, Samuel S.,	Holly	691

Proprietors.	Avenue.	Lot No.
Sleuman, Andrew,	Jessamine	694
Saltonstall, Mrs. Mary E.,	Aspen	724
Southwick, James R.,	Columbine	746
Stedman, Martha,	Ridge	756
Scott, Francis,	Violet	759
Silsbee, Rebecca A.,	Columbine	769
Saul, John,	Yew	779
Stanley, John,	Holly	782
Skerry, Robert,	Pine	790
Shreve, George C.,	Eglantine	794
Spiller, John P.,	Summit	795
Southwick, Stephen A.,	Highland	807
Smith, John R.,	Holly	829
Searle, Joseph,	Maple	833
Staten, E. H.,	Halidon	836
Smith, George G ,	Jessamine	851
Safford, John B. & Thos. R.,	Ridge	856
Saunders, Lucy L.,	Halidon	858
Symonds, Thomas Jr.,	Greenwood	880
Stowe, Volney C.,	Violet	889
Shepard, Samuel,	Jessamine	895
Saul, Joseph,	Forest	896
Shaw, X. H.,	Jessamine	900
Smith, Francis E.,	Greenwood	916
Stanley, Abraham J.,	Forest	923
Skinner, John D.,	Forest	927
Safford, Elizabeth E.,	Ridge	944

Proprietors.	Avenue.	Lot No.
Spinney, Hiram,	Halidon	946
Symonds, Robert S. D.,	Beech	983
Snow, Alice P.,	Halidon	997
Sherman, J. L.,	Forest	1009
Savory, George,	Greenwood	1021
Safford, James O.,	Greenwood	1040
Spalding, Josiah,	Eglantine	1045
Slueman, Benjamin H.,	Holly	1058
Smith, Daniel T.,	Mulberry	1064
Sanborn, F. T.,	"	1074
Sutton, William,	Linden	1083
Sutton, Ebenezer,	"	1083
Tucker, Ichabod,	Chapel	24
Taylor, Thomas B.,	Dell	27
Teel, Charles C.,	Anemone	82
Thompson, James W.,	Meadow	146
Tucker, Samuel,	Dell	160
Thorndike, William D.,	Primrose	167
Turner, J H., H. F., & C. W.,	Grove	178
Tuttle, Nathaniel,	Valley	188
Tilton, Samuel D.,	Columbine	200
Thompson, J.,	Anemone	211
Trask, Thomas,	Violet	229
Tifft, Alanson W.,	Rosemary	253
Tibbetts, Eleazer,	Violet	365
True, Abraham,	Oak	370

BUFFORD'S LITH. BOSTON.

MEADOW AV., LOOKING WEST.

XXXI

Proprietors.	Avenue.	Lot No.
Tuttle, Mrs. Sarah,	Primrose	371
Towne, Stephen F.,	Myrtle	377
Teague, Thomas A.,	Sassafras	525
Teague, Thomas A. Jr.,	"	526
Tufts, Charles H.,	Daisy	552
Towne, Henry,	Highland	589
Treadwell, Nathaniel R.,	"	596
True, Joseph,	Cowslip	614
Thorndike, Larkin,	Violet	669
Tripp, Seth D.,	Holly	673
Trask, Joseph,	Cowslip	721
Tibbets, Henry & Sarah H.,	Hemlock	737
Trumbull, Edward H.,	Gentian	764
Tabour, William,	Ridge	791
Todd, John E. A.,	"	804
Trofatter, Elias A. & W. N.,	Violet	816
Thurston, Henry W.,	Eglantine	844
Thompson, George I.,	Forest	921
Taylor, Susan,	Forest	926
Tufts, Samuel C.,	"	929
Towle, Abraham,	"	941
Towne, J. Hardy,	Halidon	961
Turner, George,	Woodbine	970
Tanch, John,	Cypress	1006
Thurston, James,	Yew	1072
Tucker, Jonathan,	Halidon	1078
Thompson, Abigail.	Woodbine	1089

Proprietors.	Avenue.	Lot No.
Thurston, H. W.,	Eglantine	1090
Upton, Luther,	Chapel	10
Upham, Charles W.,	Anemone	132
Upton, Edwin,	Halidon	364
Upton, Eben,	Jessamine	536
Upton, Moses T.,	Holly	661
Upton, George,	Gentian	692
Upton, Henry B.,	Columbine	746
Upton, James,	Highland	761
Upton, W. A.,	Holly	859
Upton, Edmund A.,	Cypress	925
Very, John,	Valley	113
Very, Nathaniel,	Aster	123
Vincent, William B.,	Chapel	287
Varney, Wm., Dan'l, & Solomon,	Eglantine	314
Very, Samuel, Jr.,	Chapel	400
Vanderford, Elizabeth,	Eglantine	496
Very, Samuel,	Jessamine	569
Very, Martha N.,	Spruce	695
Very, Nathaniel Jr.,	Angelica	698
Victory, James,	Clematis	705
Vincent, Amos L.,	Greenwood	882
Very, Nathaniel,	Forest	914
Victorato, Constantine,	Yew	1027

Proprietors.	Avenue.	Lot No.
Wright, Peter E.,	Chapel	32
Webb, Stephen,	Magnolia	40
Webb, William	Gentian	45
Wheatland, Richard G. & Benj.,	Anemone	53
Wheatland, George & Henry,	"	53
Waters, R. P. & John G.,	Iris	55
Winchester, Jacob,	Gentian	76
Wilkins, Albert,	Valley	92
Williams, J. Jr.,	Anemone	97
Ward, Andrew & Israel Jr.,	Valley	122
Webster, John,	Chapel	138
Wheatland, Richard,	Amaranth	143
Warner, Caleb,	Iris	159
Whitmore, Stephen,	Primrose	162
Walton, Timothy,	Sylvan	176
Wead, Charles W.,	Primrose	182
Wilkins, William B.,	Anemone	190
White, D. A.,	Chapel	212
Wilson, Edward,	Grove	214
Whipple, Matthew J.,	Gentian	217
Winn, Joseph,	Columbine	223
Webber, Josiah,	Primrose	239
Worcester, S. M. and J. F.,	Valley	248
Whittemore, Samuel,	Highland	250
Weeks, William,	Grove	258
Walton, George M.,	Primrose	277
Warden, John,	Highland	279

Proprietors.	Avenue.	Lot No.
Wiggin, Nathaniel,	Highland	285
Wallis, Joseph,	Primrose	321
Weir, Daniel P.,	Eglantine	325
Ward, James, *et al.*,	Summit	340
Wyman, Edward, Jr.,	Grove	378
West, George,	Violet	382
Webb, John F.,	"	382
Williams, Mehitable O.,	Rosemary	385
Whiting, Asa,	Halidon	389
Weston, Robert,	Angelica	391
Wardwell, John S.,	Chestnut	406
Whipple, Jonathan,	Violet	407
Walton, E. and E. N.,	Halidon	413
Wiihr, Lawrence W.,	Highland	425
Wallis, Hannah,	Halidon	435
Watson, Thomas R.,	"	436
Welch, Thomas T.,	Sassafras	473
Ware, Benjamin P.,	River	481
Ware, Erastus,	"	482
Ware, Horace 2d,	"	483
Walker, Abbot,	Violet	532
Wheeler, Asa,	Halidon	553
Williams, Mrs. Priscilla,	Ridge	581
Wilkins, John G.,	Jessamine	591
Webster, Daniel B.,	Ridge	594
Ward, Alfred A.,	Jessamine	628
Walton, Timothy,	Sylvan	631

BUFFORD'S LITH. BOSTON.

RECEIVING TOMB.

XXXII.

Proprietors.	Avenue.	Lot No.
Whipple, John,	Highland	634
Whipple, John H.,	"	641
Ward, William R. L.,	Locust	677
Warner, Joseph A.,	Clematis	693
Ward, Israel P.,	Meadow	702
Whipple, Henry,	Halidon	708
Wilson, Jacob,	Holly	727
Whitcomb, Israel P.,	Spruce	732
Ward, Andrew,	Summit	748
Ward, Charles,	"	754
Williams, Charles F.,	Laurel	757
Wellman, Abigail,	Hemlock	770
Whipple, Charles H.,	Laurel	802
Walker, Parker D.,	Jessamine	809
Woodbury, Caroline,	Spruce	813
Waters, John,	Cowslip	815
Warner, John V.,	"	841
Warner, Edward L.,	"	841
Williams, Mary P.,	Rosemary	862
Winchester, Percy L. & Geo. J.,	Yew	872
Winchester, Isaac,	Holly	873
Willard, Anna B.,	Halidon	881
Warner, William,	Spruce	932
Weeks, Mary E.,	Forest	939
Webber, Ira J.,	"	940
Winn, Marcia H.,	Greenwood	957
Weston, Charles,	Woodbine	979

Proprietors.	Avenue.	Lot No
West, Benjamin A.,	Greenwood	1020
Walden, Joseph F.,	Linden	1023
Webb, John K.,	Beech	1037
Webb, Eliza A.,	"	1038
Webb, Mrs. Mercy,	"	1039
Wright, Margaret,	Forest	1057
Weston, Charles,	Cypress	1082
Young, Lucy C.,	Halidon	602

OFFICERS

OF

Harmony Grove Corporation.

1866.

President.

JOSEPH S. CABOT.

Trustees.

JOSEPH S. CABOT.
FRANCIS PEABODY,
JOHN C. LEE,
GEORGE WHEATLAND,
W. H. FOSTER.
NATHANIEL SILSBEE,
E. A. HANSON,
J. W. PEELE.

Secretary and Treasurer.

W. H. FOSTER.

Superintendent.

CHARLES CREESY.

At the annual meeting of the Proprietors of the Harmony Grove Corporation, held January 3d, 1866, the following vote was passed unanimously:—

Voted, That the Lot on Greenwood Avenue, where it unites with Mulberry Avenue, be conveyed to WILLIAM H. FOSTER; and that Joseph S. Cabot, William Sutton, and Francis Peabody be a committee to see that the same is properly prepared for a burial place, and to erecting thereon a suitable monument, which shall stand as a memorial of the invaluable services rendered gratuitously by him to the Cemetery.

www.ingramcontent.com/pod-product-compliance
Lightning Source LLC
LaVergne TN
LVHW021411110826
845150LV00007B/1873